Mother Teresa, CEO

Unexpected Principles for Practical Leadership

Ruma Bose
Lou Faust

EasyRead Large

Copyright Page from the Original Book

Mother Teresa, CEO

Berrett-Koehler Publishers, Inc.
235 Montgomery Street, Suite 650
San Francisco, California 94104-2916
Tel: (415) 288-0260, Fax: (415) 362-2512
www.bkconnection.com

Ordering information for print editions
Quantity sales. Special discounts are available on quantity purchases by corporations, associations, and others. For details, contact the "Special Sales Department" at the Berrett-Koehler address above.
Individual sales. Berrett-Koehler publications are available through most bookstores. They can also be ordered directly from Berrett-Koehler: Tel: (800) 929-2929; Fax: (802) 864-7626; www.bkconnection.com
Orders for college textbook/course adoption use. Please contact Berrett-Koehler: Tel: (800) 929-2929; Fax: (802) 864-7626.
Orders by U.S. trade bookstores and wholesalers. Please contact Ingram Publisher Services, Tel: (800) 509-4887; Fax: (800) 838-1149; E-mail: customer.service@ingrampublisherservices.com; or visit www.ingram publisherservices.com/Ordering for details about electronic ordering.

Berrett-Koehler and the BK logo are registered trademarks of Berrett-Koehler Publishers, Inc.

First Edition
Hardcover print edition ISBN 978-1-60509-951-4
PDF e-book ISBN 978-1-60509-952-1
IDPF e-book ISBN 978-1-60509-953-8

2011-1

Jacket designer: Cassandra Chu
Ruma Bose photo by Sandi Fellman. Lou Faust photo by Jill Vincent.
Copyediting: Lynn Golbetz
Interior design and composition: Leigh McLellan Design

TABLE OF CONTENTS

More Praise for Mother Teresa, CEO

"Numerous articles and books have been written about Mother Teresa the humanitarian. Most of these have been focused on the impact she has had on millions of lives and not on her leadership skills that played an integral role in making her one of the most successful humanitarians of our generation. This book distills her journey into leadership principles that are easy to understand and emulate."

—William H.C. Chang, Chair, Westlake International Group, and owner, DC United and the San Francisco Giants

"*Mother Teresa, CEO* is an important contribution to the emerging paradigm of 21st-century leadership. Bose and Faust have captured the essence of her leadership success in a compelling read that gives each of us practical ideas for leading our organizations. If success is the scorecard, Mother Teresa's principles are a must-read!"

—William S. Thompson, former CEO, PIMCO

"This book is a wonderful addition to Mother Teresa's legacy. A fantastic journey that gave me insight into simple principles that can be profitably applied to any organization. Bose and Faust reveal a previously unrecognized facet of this extraordinary woman's life, one that provides lessons any leader can benefit from. Profound, engaging, and packed with insight. I couldn't recommend it more highly."

—Gloria Nelund, cofounder, Chair, and CEO, TriLinc Global, and former head, Private Wealth Management Division for North America, Deutsche Bank

"Mother Teresa inspired people throughout the world as a result of her work. She truly was an extraordinary person. This book looks at her work through the lens of her leadership for the very first time. The principles put forth by Bose and Faust provide leaders in any organization a framework for ethical and effective leadership in today's tumultuous environment. Read it. Apply the principles and you and your organization will be on your way to becoming extraordinary."

—Robert White, founder and CEO, Extraordinary People, and author of *Living an Extraordinary Life*

"All CEOs require leadership skills; however, remarkable CEOs see every roadblock as a business ramp. Bose and Faust have identified a woman who was able to exemplify these leadership principles on the global stage. A required addition to any library."

—**Gary Schwartz, CEO, Impact Mobile, Inc.**

Author Ruma Bose with Mother Teresa, Calcutta, 1992

This book is dedicated to the two angels in my life,

Mother Teresa

and my late father, Tapan Kumar Bose

RUMA

To my late mother, JoAnn Devane Faust

LOU

Preface

What Organization founded by a lone entrepreneur grew to become one of the largest enterprises in the world?

This organization was started in 1948 with a passionate leader at its helm and twelve loyal team members. Today, it:[1]

- conducts operations in over one hundred countries;
- has a loyal full-time workforce of four thousand;
- has over one million volunteer team members;
- is one of the most recognized brands in the world; and
- has raised and deployed billions of dollars in capital.

Is it Hewlett-Packard?

Is it Coca-Cola?

Is it Disney?

No, it's Mother Teresa's Missionaries of Charity.

One woman used her drive, determination, faith, and singular management style to build one of the largest orga nizations in the world. It has delivered the kind of measurable impact that most companies can only dream of achieving.

How did this nun, with no formal business training, create a global brand, a powerful fund-raising entity, and a worldwide organization over the course of forty-seven years?

Mother Teresa did what many successful entrepreneurs with great ideas do—she applied her ethical principles and values to work she was passionate about. When we view Mother Teresa from a leadership perspective, a wonderful story emerges, one filled with inspiration and life lessons.

Ruma Bose spent time in Calcutta (now Kolkata) working as a volunteer with Mother Teresa and her Missionaries of Charity in 1992. Over time, Ruma discovered that their operational success resulted from the careful application of simple but unexpected principles. Scaling an organization into over one hundred countries is not easy and doesn't happen by accident. What Mother Teresa accomplished ranks among the great business achievements in human history. Mother Teresa did not fit into a typical box, and she did not have a traditional leadership style. As a result, this book is not a typical business book. Nor is it a religious book. Instead, it will give you the unique opportunity to live Ruma's experience with Mother Teresa, learn the universal principles employed by her and her Missionaries of Charity, and discover how these principles apply, whether you are running an organization, a single project, or your everyday life. The eight principles are:

The eight principles are:

PRINCIPLE 1	Dream it simple, say it strong
PRINCIPLE 2	To get to the angels, deal with the devil
PRINCIPLE 3	Wait! Then pick your moment
PRINCIPLE 4	Embrace the power of doubt
PRINCIPLE 5	Discover the joy of discipline
PRINCIPLE 6	Communicate in a language people understand
PRINCIPLE 7	Pay attention to the janitor

PRINCIPLE 8   Use the power of silence

You may be a first-time manager, the CEO of an established company, or the founder of a start-up. You may be working with a for-profit company, a nonprofit, a nongovernmental organization (NGO), or a government organization, or you may be running a household. These timeless principles apply regardless of the type of organization. They will help you be a better leader and improve your organization's performance.

All of us can use these insights. You don't need to be a saint to benefit from Mother Teresa's example. Her influence has led us to a higher standard of leadership, and we hope it will raise your own bar too. If this book can touch your life, whether in an extraordinary or a simple way, and you can have a positive influence on the lives of others, then it will have accomplished its purpose.

INTRODUCTION

The Teresa Principles

Love is a fruit in season at all times, and within reach of every hand.

MOTHER TERESA

Ruma's story: My love for Mother Teresa began when I was a little child living in a small town outside of Montreal. My mom told me bedtime stories about this saint living in Calcutta. Each story held a lesson on the importance of faith and gratitude, service and love. Every night I looked forward to hearing the continued adventures of this "super angel." One very cold evening, I saw an old man going through our garbage, and I didn't understand why. My mom explained that some people were not as fortunate as we were. I felt an overwhelming sense of unfairness, so I decided to write Mother Teresa a letter asking her what I could do. A few months later, I received a letter back. She told me the poor are wonderful people. She told me to pray for peace and love for the old man, and to smile at him. "The more you smile and love your neighbors, the more love will spread." That letter had a profound impact on me.

Although my family was Hindu, I later graduated from the Sacred Heart School for Girls and studied at a Catholic college, all while living with two thousand nuns at the Mother House of the Grey Nuns in Montreal. Those sisters who truly loved and lived their faith inspired me and became true examples of living your passion. I kept quotes from Mother Teresa in my school agenda to inspire me daily, and she was often the topic of my high school and college essays. I was inspired by acts of service and helping others. They made me feel valued. At the time, I had a heart filled with love for others, yet very little for myself. I had my own personal struggles, and it seemed so much easier to channel the pain of growing up into doing charitable work and being idealistic. Life at nineteen, after a year of college, felt overwhelming. I was filled with both disillusionment and idealism. The desire to escape and the seduction of saving the world were calling me. So I did the only thing I knew how: I fled. I packed my bags and took a trip to India with an open heart and a rebellious mind to "find myself." I went to Calcutta to meet Mother Teresa.

After a thirty-hour journey halfway across the world, I made my way to 54A A.J.C. Bose Road to the Convent of the Missionaries of Charity. As I drove past the slums and poverty that defined the lives of so many in this city, I felt a sense of peace within it all. When I arrived at the motherhouse, I was summoned into a small room with a simple table in the middle. I could smell the humidity from the monsoons per meating the wood. As I heard footsteps in the corridor, butter flies began to stir within me.

The moment Mother entered the room, I realized why people described her presence as a life-changing experience. She may have been all of four feet eleven, but her incredible spiritual glow radiated through her being. I suddenly felt naked, with all my imperfections exposed. My vulnerability rendered me speechless. This is the closest I've ever come to an out-of-body experience. She felt like God. As she saw my over-whelmed expression, she smiled and said, "What is your name?" And there began my relationship with Mother Teresa in Calcutta.

Fifteen years later, I found myself at a similar juncture—disillusioned by my experience with the corporate world, yet still believing in the idealism of my youth. I had done many interesting things, from international marketing to international banking. I was well educated, with an MBA. Most people would have said I was a successful professional. Yet I felt I was living an empty lie. So I started looking for my new recipe for success. As I began exploring and studying different theories and models and speaking to mentors to look for inspiration, I became introspec-tive and looked into my past. As the searching got deeper, I gained a different perspective and developed a different lens through which to evaluate my life. This brought tremendous clarity on the impact of my year with Mother Teresa.

At the end of my time with her, she gave me her greatest personal gift. When I went to say good-bye, she enveloped my hand in hers and looked deeply at me with those luminous brown eyes. She spoke softly and had a wonderful way of making you feel like the most important person in the world. "We all have a purpose in life," she told me. "Some people are born to make a difference to one person, and some people are born to make a difference to their families or their countries." Then she pressed her hands more tightly onto mine. "You, Ruma, are meant to make a difference to the world. Go find your vehicle, and don't give up."

Wow! I was so afraid of those words and the empowerment they gave me. How could I translate them into something meaningful for myself and the world? I couldn't imagine that someone like me could possibly make an impact on the world. I was left speechless, but her message kept reminding me that I did have a purpose, and that if I took the time to explore it, it could manifest as something profound, transformative, and much greater than I was. The ingredients for success were always in my own experience, waiting to be discovered.

That time finally arrived a decade and a half later. A fire ignited in my soul, and I dared to dream again. I embraced the empowerment this time and decided that my vehicle was to start my own company in an industry that served those who were forgotten. I applied all the lessons learned from Mother Teresa and cofounded a floor-finishing company in the janitorial services industry. This began a new journey filled with passion, impact, and purpose. Everyone thought I was crazy—*janitorial services?* But for me, it was about what 80 percent gross margins could do for people if some of those profits were redistributed to workers. It was about valuing employees in an industry where no one did, and providing them with training and benefits and profit sharing. With passion and determination, my cofounders and I built a team and grew our operations to two hundred people and twenty-three offices nationally. My biggest rewards were watching people begin to believe in themselves and seeing people's standard of living improve. At last I understood what Mother Teresa was saying. Like many startup stories that begin with great success, the ending was less favorable than we had expected. We lost sight of the principles and vision that drove us to start the company in the first place. I spent many years reflecting on that journey, so as to avoid repeating similar management mistakes in the future. The lessons I learned through this process were a gift to me, they impacted me tremendously and helped me in my future business career.

So why this book?

Almost twenty years after my time with Mother Teresa (where did the time go?), I was conversing over pasta with a small group of people, including Richard Murphy, then the editor of *Fortune Small Business.* He asked me about my background and what inspired me. My time with Mother Teresa was such a profound and meaningful experience, one cherished so deep in my heart, that I didn't often bring it up in conversation. It was very private, something I could not share until the time was right. That time was between the salad and the ravioli on June 16, 2009. Richard asked me, "What was Mother Teresa's leadership style like?" That question ultimately led me to write this book with my mentor, Lou Faust. Completing the book has proved to be an important part of my purpose. So, thank you, Richard, for shifting my lens to view Mother Teresa from a leadership perspective, which allowed this wonderful story to emerge and be shared.

Lou's story: I was working late one night when my telephone suddenly interrupted me. Before I could finish saying hello, an excited voice yelled out, "Lou! Lou! You'll never believe the conversation I had today! I was at lunch with the editor of *Fortune Small Business* and..." I don't think she stopped to take a breath before she ended with, "He asked me if I'd be interested in writing an article on the management secrets of Mother Teresa! Can you believe that?" It was clear to me in that moment that a great idea had been born. I let her finish her story and catch her breath, and with a smile, I said, "Ruma, don't write the article. Write the book."

"Really? A book? That's a great idea! But I don't know the first thing about writing a book! Well, if I write this book, then you have to write this book with me. Deal?"

Her enthusiasm was so contagious that I didn't realize what I was signing up for when I said "Yes."

But almost two years later, I'm glad I did. The result of that conversation is the book you are holding.

I have more than thirty years of business experience, including ten on Wall Street at Salomon Brothers. I've worked in New York, San Francisco, Tokyo, and many places in between. I have held management positions in large companies and have made my own photocopies in start-ups. I've been the CEO of three institutionally funded companies. I only wish I had had the leadership principles you are about to learn when I started my career. They would have made my life and the lives of the people I was trying to lead a whole lot easier and better!

This book will give you a leadership framework that you can use every day as you confront the challenges you face, both personal and professional. When you commit to these principles and apply them consistently, they will make a positive difference in your life and to your organization.

This book is not meant to be an exhaustive analysis of how Mother Teresa ran the Missionaries of Charity. That is a very different book and one we will leave for others. Instead, it is built around simple stories that we hope will inspire you and demonstrate the eight leadership principles that led Mother Teresa and the Missionaries of Charity to build one of the most successful organizations in the world.

You, the reader, will now have the opportunity to hear the story that Ruma shared for many hours at lunch that fateful afternoon in answer to the question, "What was Mother Teresa's leadership style like?"

Enjoy the journey.

Major Milestones in Mother Teresa's Life

1910	Born in Skopje, Macedonia
1928	Joins the Sisters of Loreto in Dublin, Ireland
1929	Arrives in India
1931	Began teaching at St. Mary's High School in Calcutta
1946	Receives divine vision of Missionaries of Charity
1948	Begins Missionaries of Charity; enters Calcutta slums on December 21
1950	Vatican officially recognizes Society of the Missionaries of Charity
1952	Creates Home for the Dying
1958	Builds first mission outside Calcutta, in Drachi, India
1962	Receives the Padma Shri award for distinguished service
1963	Begins Missionaries of Charity Brothers
1965	Builds first mission outside India, in Venezuela
1971	Receives John Paul XXIII Peace Prize
1979	Receives Nobel Peace Prize
1980	Receives Bharat Ratna Award
1983	Suffers heart attack
1985	Receives the U.S. Medal of Freedom
1997	Dies
2003	Beatified by the Vatican

CHAPTER ONE

Dream It Simple, Say It Strong

To serve the poorest of the poor...

MOTHER TERESA

The power of dreams has led humans to accomplish great things. Gandhi dreamed of freedom through peace. Martin Luther King, Jr. dreamed of racial equality. Terry Fox dreamed of a cure for cancer. They didn't all have special privileges growing up, but somehow they all gained the self-confidence to dare and turn their dreams into their life missions.

Mother Teresa is one of those humans who had a simple dream that profoundly changed our world. Her dream was helping the poorest of the poor. She began with that vision, then developed a clear plan for making it come true.

Everything Mother Teresa did in her life stemmed from defining her vision and aligning and rallying all of her resources and supporters to her goal. The sisters knew what the Missionaries of Charity stood for, the poor who were served knew what the Missionaries of Charity stood for, and the world at large knew what the Missionaries of Charity stood for, whether it agreed with the vision or not.

Mother Teresa's Path

In 1928, an eighteen-year-old Albanian girl who was passionate about God joined the convent of the Sisters of Loreto. The order sent her to Calcutta to teach at a Catholic school for girls, and Calcutta introduced her to abject poverty.

Living that experience every day gave her insight into a group of people that were forgotten. She learned to understand their needs. She wanted to help the destitute and rejected, but her experience allowed her to refine where and how the help was most needed and could have the most effect. She realized over time that her true purpose was not to help at a broad level, but to help a very specific group of people who could not help themselves and whom others forgot about.

In 1946, Mother Teresa heard these important insights as a direct call from God. She realized that she needed not only to change her own path in life, but to form a separate congregation that focused on helping the destitute. She could not accomplish her vision while staying with the Sisters of Loreto. Thus, in what she described as a more difficult sacrifice than leaving her family to join the convent, she made the decision to bid farewell to that second family, which she had loved dearly for over twenty years, and asked the pope for special permission to start a new religious order called the Missionaries of Charity.

The founding of a new order was not easy and took four years from the time she received her vision. Moreover, when Mother Teresa left the Sisters of Loreto, she had only five hundred rupees in her pocket. But she was not going to let either bureaucracy or finances get in her way. She recruited twelve nuns to join her, and together they opened a school in the slums of Calcutta in 1948. They spent the next three years managing, learning, and growing their little school to capacity. In October 1950, the Vatican gave Mother Teresa permission to start her own order.

Its mission, in Mother Teresa's own words, was to care for "the hungry, the naked, the homeless, the crippled, the blind, the lepers, all those people who feel unwanted, unloved, uncared for throughout society, people that have become a burden to the society and are shunned by everyone."[2]

The sisters saw the direct impact their work had on children and diligently embarked on a growth trajectory to broaden that impact. They first expanded locally in Calcutta. Their first hospice was an abandoned Hindu temple named Kalighat Home for the Dying, later renamed Nirmal Hriday (Pure Heart), a free hospice for the poor. Soon they opened a home for lepers, Shanti Nagar (City of Peace). Ten years after their founding, the Missionaries of Charity had established homes for lepers, orphanages, and hospices throughout India.[3]

In 1965, Mother Teresa asked Pope Paul VI to allow her order to expand into other countries. Permission was granted, and the order opened its first house outside of India, in Venezuela. Others followed in Rome, in Tanzania, and eventually throughout Africa, Asia, and Europe. At the time of Mother Teresa's death, forty-seven years after she started the order, she was operating 594 missions in more than one hundred countries, with over one million coworkers.[4] She was a PR magnet and had raised and deployed billions of dollars in capital. Her human impact and track record are unsurpassed to this day.

Mother Teresa's vision timelessly lives on. She became the vision and an iconic symbol of service to the poor. It took her twenty years to realize the beginning of her dream, then a lifetime to achieve it and let the world hear it—simple, loud, and clear.

Vision

Great business leaders, like Mother Teresa, start with a simple vision they can evangelize internally and externally. Simplicity and strength of message are essential. The vision needs to be set up early, even before you start your company. Mother Teresa had the vision of serving the poorest of the poor before she founded the Missionaries of Charity. Her personal vision became the vision for the organization.

Your vision comes from your lived experiences and beliefs. Twenty years of exposure to poverty taught Mother Teresa the importance of serving the underserved in particular ways. Can you imagine the young Bill Gates setting up an organization like the one Mother Teresa did? It would have been terribly difficult because Bill Gates did not have her direct understanding of poverty. However, he was at the right spot to start a company in what he did understand that grew 30 percent yearly for over two decades; then he donated much of his wealth.

As a leader you should ask yourself, "What are you a Mother Teresa of?" A simple vision can create the momentum to build or move mountains, as Mother Teresa did.

To identify a personal vision requires introspection. We need to listen to ourselves, determine by our actions what we value, and take the time to understand who we truly are or what we are trying to be. Once we understand our core values, the key is to distill those values into a simple vision.

Dreaming It Simple

Simplicity makes a vision powerful. Mother Teresa was crystal clear about where she would focus her organization's resources: at the lowest level of the poverty pyramid. We all have roles to play in the world, as individuals and in our organizations. A person's world may be focused on family, community, work, or a cause. Once you understand personally what your role is, you can begin creating the road map to align all aspects of your efforts.

"Simple," however, does not mean "oversimplified." When crafting the visions for their organizations, many leaders go through a lengthy, collaborative process. The result can be a "kitchen sink vision" that tries to address current management buzzwords but does not reflect the true core of the company. We have all seen examples like these:

Our people are our greatest asset.

Our goal is quality.

We deliver world-class service.

These generic "visions" are not specific enough to be actionable or attainable in our lives or by our organizations. The words have no real meaning. With a simple vision, each word matters.

Saying It Strong

"Saying it strong" speaks to the constant need for a leader to consistently speak with passion and conviction about her vision for her organization. She also must act in ways aligned with that vision. A well-articulated vision cannot realize its transformational potential if it is left in a corporate planning binder on the CEO's shelf, never seeing the light of day until the next year's planning process, if then.

The Missionaries of Charity were there to serve the poorest of the poor, and they lived their lives in the simple manner of those they served. Mother Teresa understood her customer, and this was reflected in everything she did: her simple attire of a white sari with three blue stripes, reflecting her vows of chastity, poverty, and obedience; her simple living quarters; and her even simpler way of life. She lived the values she preached. This alignment between vision and action enabled people to believe in her and gave her the authenticity to support the worldwide growth of the Missionaries of Charity.

RUMA'S STORY: When I first met Mother Teresa, she was already famous throughout the world. Whether you were from New York City, a village in Brazil, or the countryside in Cambodia, you knew who Mother Teresa was. Yet the simplicity of her conduct stood out immediately. The moment you met her, you knew this was a visionary who was living to serve the poor. Her environment, her clothing, her language, her demeanor all said, "I am serving the poorest of the poor." The message was simple, loud, and clear.

Mother Teresa did not have to use a lengthy or formal process to roll out her vision to the Missionaries of Charity. She simply led by example, living a life consistent with her vision. By living what she believed, she inspired others to follow her. She articulated a vision for her organization, then talked about it and acted on it every possible moment. In other words, she dreamed it simple and said it strong!

LOU'S STORY: The year 2001 was tumultuous for technology companies in the United States, and many companies and founders were left with shattered dreams and empty bank accounts. The software company of which I was the president was no exception. Although we managed to survive, times were tough. One Monday, the CEO informed me she was leaving. The board of directors immediately asked me to become the interim CEO while they searched for a replacement. I knew this would not be an easy task. The company had to be united and focused on a common vision for its future in order to weather the storm. To do this right and get everyone aligned, I created a team of people who were well respected within the organization. The team members listened to and discussed and debated with other people in the company as well as each other.

As the leader of the organization, however, I did not abdicate ultimate responsibility for the vision. The leader needs to put a process in place and then stay involved, providing guidance and keeping the process on track to achieve the established goals. The team's initial suggestions were too vague and didn't reflect that the company wanted to achieve specific results. Because this was a for-profit company, its long-term viability and success would be functions, in large part, of its financial results. I needed to keep that idea in front of everyone in the organization. Consequently, I directed the team to think about how to best incorporate that focus into the corporate values. This collaborative process resulted in a vision statement and a set of values that embraced the collective voice.

The team's work was rolled out to the entire organization at a company-wide meeting, followed by additional smaller meetings. There was, as expected, initial skepticism. Previous efforts to develop a lasting vision had failed. We have all seen this before in companies: the "vision of the month." We avoided this as well as the kitchen sink vision by actively engaging people in creating the vision and by testing it at every stage. Finally, to address the skepticism, we needed to build the vision and values into how we ran the company.

As the CEO, I incorporated the new vision into my daily routine and began to emphasize its core messages, both internally in meetings with the executive team, lunch meetings with employees, and new-employee orientations, and externally with customers and prospects. It became part of how I did my job every day. Over time, the buy-in spread through the company and became part of the culture as more and more stakeholders began to live the values daily, just as they had witnessed their leader do.

Leadership

You as the leader have the ultimate responsibility to determine the purpose and vision of your organization. What is your vision? Can you state it clearly? Is it simple? Do you believe in it? Do you live it? Does it motivate you every day? Has your organization incorporated it into the way it works?

As a leader, you are the voice of the vision. You must continually seek out opportunities to seamlessly weave your vision into your daily routine, such as meetings with customers or employees. You must keep the vision front and center and use it as a touchstone against which you and everyone else in the organization make decisions, large and small. This real-world application gives visibility to your vision and makes it real for everyone in the organization. It can transform it from words on the wall (we have all seen these posters on company walls) to words in the heart of everyone in the organization.

Your ability to act in ways clearly aligned with the orga nization's vision will accelerate its adoption by everyone in the organization. It also will provide a model of behavior that people can use as they do their work every day. The accretive power of a shared vision with organizational alignment will yield measurable results.

Mother Teresa first articulated her vision "to serve the poorest of the poor" for the Missionaries of Charity nearly sixty years ago. It has the strength of passion radiating from seven simple words. It is aspirational. The results speak for themselves. The Missionaries of Charity today is an iconic global organization with operations in 134 countries on five continents. Its enduring power is a function of the simplicity and strength of its vision. Dreamed simple, said strong!

THE TERESA PRINCIPLES

Dream It Simple, Say It Strong
- Dare to dream
- Be passionate about what you seek to be and achieve
- Articulate a clear, simple vision for yourself or your organization
- Demonstrate both the vision and the values in all that you do

CHAPTER TWO

To Get to the Angels, Deal with the Devil

*If you are humble, nothing will touch you,
neither praise nor disgrace,
because you know what you are.*

MOTHER TERESA

Imagine the business that has been in your family for fifty years is days away from running out of cash. You have three hundred employees and their families relying on their jobs to provide for them. Your uncle has served time in prison and embarrassed the family for years but has offered to bail you out. You have no other alternatives. What do you do?

This story and others like it represent an ethical dilemma that each of us may face at some point, be it in a personal or a professional setting. It is at these times that our values shine and our stress levels skyrocket. You are a leader; you have spent the last few years building your vision; how far are you willing to stretch for it? Does the end justify the means? What is important in these situations is to understand what your goal is and then to recognize where you draw your line. What would you do in this situation?

The Devil

Here's a conclusion to a similar story. Mother Teresa and the Missionaries of Charity accepted money from the notorious Jean-Claude "Baby Doc" Duvalier, the ruler of Haiti.[5] Baby Doc was driven into exile because of his repressive regime and his brutal treatment of the people of his country.

It has also been reported that Mother Teresa accepted more than one million dollars from Charles Keating, the former CEO of the infamous Lincoln Savings and Loan in the United States.[6] More than twenty-three thousand people owned investments related to Lincoln, and when it collapsed, many lost their life savings. The collapse also cost the U.S. government over three billion dollars. Mr. Keating ended up serving more than four years in prison.

How could Mother Teresa possibly take money from these types of people? Wasn't it directly opposed to everything she and the Missionaries of Charity stood for? In her ethical scheme, they were "devils," but she dealt with them anyway.

Mother Teresa faced other forms of the devil throughout the growth of the Missionaries of Charity. Critics, who became increasingly vocal as her success grew, perceived downsides to her work. Some called attention to her use of donated money to open new convents and increase missionary work rather than on improving conditions at the hospices or helping to end poverty.

The Missionaries of Charity do not disclose either the sources of their funds or details of how they are spent. In 1998 an article in the German magazine *Stern* estimated that the order received about fifty million dollars a year in donations.[7] Other journalists have given estimates of one hundred million dollars a year. Critics have argued that this money cannot all have been spent on the purpose for which it was donated—aid to the sick and the poor—because the order's facilities, staffed by nuns and volunteers and offering little in the way of medical care, are very inexpensive to operate. Critics maintain that the majority of the money donated is transferred to the

Vatican Bank in Rome, where it is used by the Catholic Church for its general purposes, or to non-Christian countries for missionary work. It has also been widely said that primitive methods, rather than proper medical care, have been used to treat the poor and dying who come to the Houses of Charity.

How did Mother Teresa respond to these perceived devils—essentially the results of operating within the larger church organization, and of working on an enormous and intractable problem? By standing firm in her beliefs. As Clark Morphew, syndicated columnist for Knight-Ridder Newspapers, puts it:

> Wiping out poverty and illiteracy was not Mother Teresa's focus. She set out as a young woman to form an order that would bring a touch of humanity and the theology of the Catholic Church to the poor of the world. She never pretended to be a doctor who could wipe out or even soften the pain of death. She and her little army of sisters were there to bring spiritual comfort to the suffering, a concept that apparently escapes her critics.
>
> That said, she was human, and she surely made mistakes. But despite the terrible challenges and the opposition to her methodologies, she never gave up.[8]

Whether Mother Teresa herself identified these criticisms as "devils" or whether the problem was that being criticized made her work more difficult, we do not know. Either way, criticism did not lessen her determination to pursue her work. Mother Teresa never set out to change the world, just to help the person in front of her.

As a leader, you too will face challenges to your principles. For example, how can you do business with someone whose values are not aligned with yours? How will doing so impact your organization and its people? How will it impact your customers?

Getting to the Angels

Mother Teresa's angels were the poor people whom she served. Comforting and offering dignity to those who had never received it were her bottom line. The number of lives she touched was her return on investment. Building the global infrastructure to reach them was her biggest capital cost. Her sole source of funding was donated capital. Mother Teresa's focus never wavered from her mission to serve the poorest of the poor, and she needed money to do her work.

Devils have done terrible things to humankind. Their capital may have been gained in terrible ways. So where do you draw the line in dealing with them? Mother Teresa drew a clear line between the source of the donation and its use. She decided that the good the money could do in serving more of the poorest of the poor outweighed the character of its source. She accepted charity from the devils to get to the angels.

Choices

As a leader, you can approach ethical dilemmas by answering several questions. First, who are your angels, and what is your goal? Mother Teresa's angels were the poorest of the poor, and her goal was to serve them. To do that, she needed people and money. The Missionaries of Charity need capital to support their daily activities as well as the opening of new missions in areas of need. The organization gets this capital principally from donations.

Second, what is your guiding principle on the issue at hand? Mother Teresa believed that charity comes from the heart. Therefore, she did not question the origins of her donations. She was often quoted as saying, "If you judge people, you have no time to love them." This is a paraphrase but is entirely consistent with her beliefs as we understand them.

Finally, where in your value set do you draw the line? Knowing she was doing good things with the money given to her, Mother Teresa would take money unquestioningly, but that's as far as she would go. She never allowed donors to exploit her name or the Missionaries of Charity for their own purposes.

RUMA'S STORY: As Mother Teresa and her Missionaries of Charity grew in reputation, institutions, corporations, and multinationals often came knocking on her door to donate. More often than not, these offers of money were conditioned on commercial benefit for the donors. I remember multinationals approaching Mother and offering money in return for endorsements. Mother Teresa always refused. That was her line. She would not commercially endorse businesses.

Indeed, she would not accept payment for any services, only charity. She stated, "We never accept an invitation to eat out. Would you like to know why? Because accepting these invitations might give the impression that we accept payment for what we do, and we do everything free of charge."[9]

At the time I volunteered with the Missionaries of Charity I was thinking of applying to law school, and I thought of asking Mother Teresa for a recommendation letter. The other sisters told me she would not write recommendations for volunteers anymore. She believed our volunteer work should not be done for personal benefit, but should come from the heart.

Leaders need to know where to draw their lines. Sometimes you have to compromise. You need to have the courage to decide which compromises are acceptable and which are not. You will not always make the right choices, and you will get criticized for them. Mother Teresa was criticized about many of her choices. Her response was to stand by her beliefs and focus on getting her job done. Other leaders may have to make similar choices, and being righteous and judgmental in our views will not help. Perhaps a potential customer is known for less-than-ethical business dealings with others. Do you therefore turn down a deal with that customer? Or, as a leader with obligations to your people, do you do the deal because it will enable you to make payroll, keep your people employed, let them buy food for their families, and keep the doors open and thus further realize your company's vision?

RUMA'S STORY: I have raised a lot of money for profit and nonprofit ventures. When I pitch, I try to appeal to people's values. Sometimes, though, I face challenges similar to Mother Teresa's. I have heard that someone has done something that violates my principles—but that person is also able to write a check that will save from bankruptcy a company that employs two hundred people and helps them feed their families and put their children through school. Will taking that check compromise my principles? Which compromises are acceptable, and which are not? When do the means justify the ends?

LOU'S STORY: I was the chairman of the board of an early-stage consumer products company that was raising its first round of outside capital. The CEO did a great job in getting a term sheet from an institutional investor very quickly in a down market. However, the term sheet was extremely onesided in the investor's favor and not at all supportive of the management team. Although the money would have enabled the company to further realize its short-term goals, it would have hindered its ability to achieve its long-term vision. The CEO and founder decided, ultimately with the board's support, to reject it. The company failed to raise the capital from another source. Ultimately it sold all of its products but did not have enough capital to fund more production. All of us as individuals and as leaders will face decisions on dealing with our devils to get to our angels. How will you decide?

Mother Teresa's second leadership principle teaches us the need for a framework to make difficult ethical choices and how such a framework can help guide our decisions every single day as we lead our organizations. This second principle rests squarely on top of our first principle of "dream it simple, say it strong." Taken together, they form the foundation upon which the remaining principles are built.

THE TERESA PRINCIPLES

To Get to the Angels, Deal with the Devil
- Remember who your angels are
- Know your ethical line
- Evaluate every choice against your line
- Don't cross your line

CHAPTER THREE

Wait! Then Pick Your Moment

Yesterday is gone.
Tomorrow has not yet come.
We have only today. Let us begin.

MOTHER TERESA

HAVE YOU EVER waited twenty years to begin something? Have you ever had the patience to wait and pick your moment? Mother Teresa did. Nearly twenty years passed from her joining the Sisters of Loreto in Dublin to her starting the Missionaries of Charity in Calcutta. The road was long, and in more than just miles. Starting a new religious order within the Catholic Church is not an easy task.

Aha!

When a vision emerges from a place deep within you, and it is aligned with your core value system, you can't get it out of your mind. Suddenly, you are open to a whole new world of possibility, and your brain screams, "Aha!" Once the brain takes charge, the thought changes from "Can I?" to "I can." That is the defining moment—but it does not necessarily mean you can start right away.

Mother Teresa knew in her heart that she was meant to help the poor, but she waited to start her own unique mission until the time was right for her. The "right" time may not be convenient, but when the inspiration comes, it's important to listen. For Mother Teresa, a call from God en route to a retreat in Darjeeling enlightened her that it was time to begin what she knew she was meant to do. But those of us who don't have God's number need to pay attention to the pearls of wisdom from those around us, as well as keenly observing our own behaviors and habits.

Mother came to open a home for the dying in Kalighat after she met a woman dying on a sidewalk. She wanted to alleviate the woman's suffering and let her die with dignity by offering her a bed. Mother Teresa brought the woman with her, gave her a bed, and let her die in peace. This simple act of love led her to open the Home for the Dying.

Readiness

As a leader, once you have determined your vision, you must ask yourself a number of questions and make a number of decisions. Whether you are starting a new organization or taking leadership of an existing one, one of the first questions to ask is, "Are we ready?"

Once Mother Teresa had her vision of serving the poorest of the poor, she had to address a number of factors before being ready to move forward. She knew that her vision could not be accomplished within the existing Catholic organizations. A new order was necessary. One of her most pressing challenges was to receive authority from the church to create that order. This process was long and involved many levels of approval. She faced repeated resistance from the church hierarchy, locally and in Rome, and from the leaders of the Sisters of Loreto. Armed with a clear vision, an unrelenting focus, and unswerving commitment, she did everything they asked her to do in order to move toward her goal.

Readiness is a complex state. In the corporate world, whether you are launching a new organization or seeking to establish a new direction for an existing one, a myriad of financial, legal, and human resources requirements need to be met. In the nonprofit world in the United States, the paperwork to secure tax-exempt status for purposes of collecting donations also must be completed and filed. Governments and NGOs must meet their own often detailed requirements before embarking on new programs. Extensive public hearings and comment periods add to the time it takes to get even the simplest new government programs up and running.

How Ready Are You?

While there is no universal set of requirements to guide you in assessing your readiness to begin, there are some guidelines. There are three linked categories to consider: emotional, financial, and operational. If you or the organization falls short on any one of the three, then you must decide how to proceed. Do you decide this is not yet your moment, and continue your preparation? Or do you press ahead, recognizing that you have now changed the probability of success and the risk profile of the organization? Leadership requires understanding risk and reward when making decisions. These are threshold decisions."

Emotional readiness is the ability to successfully and rapidly adjust to constant and possibly extreme emotional swings from high highs to low lows. Emotional readiness for an individual or an organization is often challenging. For Mother Teresa it was critical. She was the catalyst for the new order. Her dogged determination enabled her to overcome the church's continued insistence that she could do her work within its existing infrastructure. Her ability to withstand its pressures and keep moving toward her vision showed that she was emotionally ready to tackle the other challenges she would face in creating and building the Missionaries of Charity.

A balance between action and reflection is critical to keep focused during the emotional ups and downs of leadership. When reflecting, ask yourself if you are moving toward your vision, laying the groundwork to ensure you are ready once the time is right. Mother Teresa used the time it took to obtain church approval to prepare herself and her organization. Thus, when she finally received the approval, she was ready, and the Missionaries of Charity was begun.

RUMA'S STORY: One of Mother Teresa's houses was Prem Dan, a long-term convalescent facility. Like the Home for the Dying, Prem Dan was a place where people had the comfort of being surrounded by love before they left this earth. The work involved was labor intensive and emotional. People were dying every day. When I first arrived, the sisters sought to make sure I was ready to deal with the emotional hardships of being around death daily. I was confident of my readiness. After all, I thought, they had told me that the people didn't need pity, but love. How difficult could that be? But I was wrong. Nothing had prepared me for this. I had the privilege of feeding, bathing, and spending time with people rejected by society and suffering alone. The experience was not only humbling, it was overwhelming. I had nightmares. I was angry with God. I didn't understand how such immense suffering could exist in our world. In short, the sisters' intuition was right—I was not ready.

Financial readiness is the ability to access enough money to move the organization forward and achieve its plan. How much is enough? The answer will vary widely, depending upon the organization. Mother Teresa started with just five hundred rupees. She struggled to raise enough capital to fund some of the earlier programs of the Missionaries of Charity. As we learned earlier, sometimes to get to the angels, she had to deal with devils.

Mother Teresa realized that the Missionaries of Charity was not financially secure when it started. However, readiness does not mean having the answer to every question and having everything exactly as you would like it. It means understanding your organization's current condition and the associated risks and then deciding it is time to act.

Mother Teresa's vision of serving the poorest of the poor compelled her to move ahead. She did so knowing her financial situation and understanding the risk. However, she had not only faith, but a plan to raise the money the organization needed to fund its operations. In contrast, entrepreneurs starting companies often exhibit blind faith. They don't understand financial readiness but are convinced they will raise the capital they need in time for everything to work out. Many never do.

LOU'S STORY: I worked for a CEO of a software company that was always trying to raise the capital it needed to grow and to realize its vision. For over eighteen months the CEO was convinced that the next big investor was going to put a lot of money into the company. However, during my time there, the company never had the money to hire the people it needed or to market its solution effectively. It was not ready. Consequently, it struggled to even keep the people it had. The big investor never came, and all but two people left the company. Those two people and the CEO worked for no pay for months. The CEO continued to raise money in small amounts, but it has never been enough to give the company a real opportunity to realize its vision.

It is almost always the CEO who must lead the effort to secure the funding necessary to move the organization toward its vision. The leader must raise this capital while continuing to provide day-to-day operational guidance. This is a difficult balance. Capital is the lifeblood of early-stage companies. Without it most will die, some more quickly than others. It is the leader's job to ensure that the company is financially ready to not only survive but thrive as it strives toward its vision. However, you also need to provide sufficient guidance to the people running daily operations to ensure the company's success.

The pursuit of capital also inevitably tests the emotional readiness of the leader. It is perhaps the best example of the emotional roller-coaster ride that is starting a new organization. You may meet a prospect who leaves you feeling excited that you will close the funding gap much faster than you had thought; in your next meeting, potential investors may tear apart what you thought was a great plan, leaving you feeling your vision is hopeless and you were crazy to think you could ever raise any money for your organization. During the pursuit of capital, your emotional stability will be tested again and again. Success will determine your readiness and the readiness of the organization to move forward.

The third major area that must be assessed is operational readiness: the ability to actually do all the necessary activities to run your organization on a daily basis and reach your vision. For instance, if you are selling a product, can you manufacture it at consistent quality in the volume you need at a cost you can afford, and can you get it to where it will be sold profitably and on a timely basis? If you are selling a service, can you deliver it when, how, and where your customer wants it, at a price the customer is willing to pay? If you are a nonprofit, can you deliver your programs at a cost low enough that you are being a good financial steward and meeting your donors' and the community's expectations? And if you are a government agency, are you delivering your services within your required budgets?

Regardless of the type of organization you are leading, a key element in assessing your operational readiness is to evaluate your team. If you don't have the right people armed with the required resources and support, operational readiness will be severely affected, and this will impair the organization's potential to succeed.

Mother Teresa clearly demonstrated operational readiness. She spent nearly twenty years working as a teacher and principal, which gave her leadership experience. She had time to observe her surroundings in Calcutta, meet with the impoverished, and recognize her dream to serve them. She put in place the team she needed. After the Missionaries of Charity began its work in Calcutta, she continually assessed her own and the organization's readiness to grow. It was ten years before she opened its first mission outside of Calcutta, in Drachi, India. It was seven teen years before she opened the first mission outside of India, in Venezuela.

Are you prepared to handle the emotional ups and downs of starting a new organization? Do you have the financial and human resources to start down this path? If you have a slow period, will you have the capital to get through it until your business improves? Finally, are you and your organization able to deliver the goods and services you tell your customers you can? Can you provide the quality and service they expect, at a price where you make the return you need to grow your business? Are you ready?

Wait, pick your moment, and go!

THE TERESA PRINCIPLES

Wait! Then Pick Your Moment

- Patience is required
- Persistence is mandatory
- Assess your readiness emotionally financially operationally
- Go!

CHAPTER FOUR

Embrace the Power of Doubt

*We ourselves feel that what we are doing
is just a drop in the ocean. But the ocean would
be less because of that missing drop.*

MOTHER TERESA

Any path worth taking will have rises and falls. These ultimately give us the strength that can only come from life experience. They also evoke a colorful set of emotions, from doubt to the desire to escape to the joy of seeing someone touched by our service. We need the ability to persevere through the difficult moments.

Mother Teresa never gave up. She persisted in the face of crippling conditions of poverty and a seemingly impossible war. She devoted her life to serving the voiceless. She saved children and families in the midst of violent civil wars around the world, whether at the height of the famine in Southern Sudan or between Hindus and Muslims in India. This is a woman who assisted the destitute in Kenya, earthquake victims in Armenia, and radiation victims at Chernobyl. She never lost sight of her mission to serve the neediest, wherever they may be found. From the slums of Calcutta to the war-torn city of Beirut, Mother Teresa persisted and provided these people with a place of peace.

One might guess that such a strong woman, with her relentless commitment to those less fortunate, never doubted herself or her path, or accepted doubt in others. Her private writings, however, tell a very different story. Yet to the outside world, there was never any question as to her commitment. Mother Teresa not only faced but embraced doubts. She just did not let them slow her down. She stood tall against her personal spiritual struggle and overwhelming feelings of loneliness. She never stopped.

Embracing the Power of Doubt

Mother Teresa's letters to her spiritual father, written in confidence, give us a rare glimpse into her deepest thoughts. She laid bare her internal struggles as she pursued her vision to serve the poorest of the poor. These letters show her questioning her faith and feeling tremendous doubt, distance from God, and spiritual isolation. She questioned the very source that brought her to her work—her relationship with God. Her belief in Jesus and the work he was doing through her had driven all her decisions. Yet working in some of the world's most impoverished environments and seeing their terrible impact on people can call faith into question. It made even Mother Teresa doubt her core beliefs.[10] She continued to doubt herself during critical times in her life as she sought to grow the Missionaries of Charity.

Doubt isn't necessarily a crisis of faith. Obstacles are a daily part of life. You can have faith that something good is going to happen, but doubt how you are ever going to get there. When we embark on journeys into the unknown, it is important to acknowledge and process our feelings of doubt. Unprocessed doubt can lead to paralyzing fear, but using doubt to question yourself can strengthen your beliefs and free you from that fear.

It is courageous to realize that not everything is without risk. Courage is the ability to persevere toward your goal in spite of fear—as Ambrose Redmoon puts it, "the judgment that something else is more important than fear."[11] Indeed, what you do with your doubt in part will determine whether or not you can reach your goal.

Mother Teresa brought her struggles to the forefront of her thinking, as we can see from her writings. This path required great personal strength and commitment to working through these issues. By accepting that doubts occur and consciously acknowledging and even embracing them, Mother Teresa developed a way to positively work with them. Indeed, her relentless questioning gave her great, enduring strength that ultimately helped her to build the Missionaries of Charity into a successful global organization. How did Mother Teresa put her doubts to use?

First, she recognized that doubt only has positive power in the context of the vision. Embracing the power of doubt does not mean doubting the vision. If you were part of the Missionaries of Charity, you were signed up to serve the poorest of the poor. Within the security of that certainty, Mother Teresa was free to embrace the power of doubt at every other level, from any source. Powerful questions could illuminate better ways of achieving the vision. However, questions asked for the sake of asking questions, or out of fear of making decisions, had to be put aside, gently but firmly, by asking another question: "How would knowing the answer to this question help us do something better, now, to achieve the dream?"

Second, she knew that doubt could be beneficial regardless of its source. Many leaders need to be seen as infallible. Their attitude is, "I'll ask the questions around here." However, it is both unfair and ineffective for the leader to do all the questioning. Mother Teresa's approach embraced each person's question as holding the key to some improvement. When others talked, she listened. If a question led to an understanding of how to do better, she acted.

Third, she embedded the power of doubt in action, not mere words. She was always on the move, except when she stopped to listen or reflect. By setting a personal example of action, making and expecting continual progress, she put doubt in its proper place—as a guide when we are uncertain, not a refuge from the responsibility to act. Mother Teresa's positive energy made it safe for her, and others, to bring their honest doubts forward. No one needed to fear that uncertainty would lead to indecision or paralysis. She embraced doubt regularly, not occasionally—and continued to act.

To put it another way, when it was time to make a call, she made it. Whether the issue was acceptance of donations from some devil or readiness to expand to a new location, once the questions had been asked and honestly answered, she took responsibility.

Processing through Questioning

Doubt is a fact of life for any honest person. The only thing we know for sure is that we don't know much. But the challenges of leadership present a dilemma. How can you embrace the power of doubt to energize the quest for the truth without crippling your organization with indecision?

Once you start facing your doubts, questioning yourself and your organization's plans, it may feel as if you will never be able to stop. Am I doing the right thing? Is there really a market here? Will customers really pay what we think they will? Do they really value our offerings? Can we make any money at these prices? How can we make these products at the cost we need to make any money? How will we find the people we need to build and grow the organization? Is our strategy sound? Are we focusing on the right problems? Will we make our numbers? Will our investors continue to support us? How committed are our top performers? What is our competition up to? And what about the economy?

These, and thousands of other questions, must be asked. And they must be answered, as best we can. And we can't limit our expressions of doubt to the safe haven of a yearly planning meeting. The world is always changing, and if we don't also doubt our plans, we will eventually pay the price of hubris.

But doubt has a price, too. It costs time, money, and emotional energy to keep questioning. And no one ever closed a deal, sold a product, raised capital, hired a superstar, or got a factory online by just asking questions. Successful leaders find courage in the face of fear so that they can lead their organizations forward. Unless the leader is willing to bear the burden of making a decision while doubt still hangs in the air, everyone will begin to fear doubt itself. Honest questioning will dry up, and good people will look elsewhere for a place to make their contributions. Having embraced doubt, the leader must finally decide as if there were no doubt at all.

Making Doubt Work

To embrace doubt productively, it is important to develop a reasoned, balanced framework and process to deal with it. The leader of any organization must continually assess its progress toward its goals, as well as question the validity of its vision in an ever-changing world. This assessment includes reviewing financial and operational successes and failures, customer and employee satisfaction, and stakeholder buy-in to the corporate vision. Are you profitable, with a clean balance sheet? What are your customer retention levels? Do you know if your customers are satisfied, and why? Are you growing your business, quarter-over-quarter, year-over-year? Is your employee turnover rate acceptable? Are you excited to be working there? Is your vision a motivating factor?

Mother Teresa started out with doubts about how she would get to where she knew she had to go, and she even doubted her faith. But she never wavered from her vision of the Missionaries of Charity, and she never gave up. As a leader, you can express in actions her principle of embracing the power of doubt to achieve strategic clarity, operational effectiveness, and organizational alignment.

LOU'S STORY: I was promoted to run global operations at one of the most powerful financial services companies in the world. It was a huge promotion, and other people were passed over for it. I had been successful in all my prior positions at the company, but this role was far more complex than any I had ever had. Many thought I would fail. I was excited but scared to death. I doubted I could do it.

I confronted my doubt directly by identifying the issues that needed to be addressed and acting on them. I chose those issues that were important to resolve in a manner consistent with what the company was trying to accomplish. By taking consistent action aligned with what we were trying to achieve, I began to get things done and started to build my credibility within the organization. As my credibility rose, my own doubt receded.

Embracing the power of doubt helped Mother Teresa realize the vision of the Missionaries of Charity. You can use this powerful leadership principle to assess whether your own organization is on a path to realizing its vision. It will also give your people confidence that you are being thoughtful in constantly evaluating the organization and making the appropriate decisions for its future.

THE TERESA PRINCIPLES

Embrace the Power of Doubt
- Embracing doubt can be very powerful
- Use doubt to gauge when to check in with your organization and yourself
- Express your doubt without communicating fear
- Embed the power of doubt in action

CHAPTER FIVE

Discover the Joy of Discipline

The miracle is not that we do this work,
but that we are happy to do it.

MOTHER TERESA

RUMA'S STORY: It was the same every morning. The alarm would ring at 5a.m. and my battle with the snooze button would begin. How much I valued those extra moments of sleep! I would lazily walk into the kitchen, boil water on the gas stove, pour it into a bucket of cold water, and use a jug to bathe. It was invariably 5:40a.m. before I rushed out the door to make it to 6a.m. Mass. Most days I was late, and one of the sisters would usher me into the back of the chapel. Mornings have always been stressful for me.

Over time, I improved. The snooze button remained my friend, but I became better at managing myself, and then a funny thing happened. The anxiety-filled ride to the motherhouse became a peaceful one. The rising sun burned off the fog; the sounds of distant morning prayers murmured through the air as shopkeepers prepared to open up on the footpaths of Lower Circular Road. I began to enjoy Calcutta for its raw beauty, in those brief twenty minutes before the cacophony that defines this city began. When I saw the big red tax building, I knew I was thirty seconds away from my destination, and I sat back, took a breath, and looked forward to the day.

The discipline and focus with which Mother Teresa lived her life were exemplary. She and the sisters were up at 4:40 every morning and assembled in the chapel for morning prayers by 5:00. Next came Mass, which volunteers and outsiders were welcome to attend. Everyone sat on the floor, sisters on one side, visitors and volunteers on the other. A few electric fans stirred the humid air. Despite the minor hardship, this eventually became my favorite part of the day. There were people from all over the world and all walks of life. On any given day, I might see a Swedish volunteer sitting next to a Japanese tourist, a Brazilian family of five, an Indian maid, a child from the slums singing at Mass, or a priest in training from Italy. There was a beautiful feeling of togetherness. A simple breakfast of chai, white bread, and bananas followed. We sang devotional songs, said a prayer, and then, by 8a.m., dutifully went into rush-hour Calcutta for a bus ride to our "jobs."

Don't Procrastinate!

Mother Teresa's schedule was grueling and demanded tremendous discipline. In a typical day she visited various centers around the city and managed the sisters at each. She regularly traveled internationally to keep in touch and be on top of the five to six hundred missions around the world. Whether she was in Baghdad, Boston, Bolivia, or Berlin, she was doing something challenging every day, every month, every year. She constantly demonstrated her leadership and discipline by getting things done in every area of her organization. She was a joyful leader by example to the sisters, to the volunteers, to the poor, and to the world.

In leadership, as in life, discipline is about doing. It's about getting out of bed at 4a.m.; it's about turning the television off and doing your homework;

it's about not eating that piece of chocolate cake on the first day of your diet; it's about completing that sales report or drafting the new marketing collateral. Discipline is about the long-term benefit. There is no shortcut or miracle pill. It takes effort and willpower to succeed at business and in life.

Procrastination is the enemy of discipline. Mother Teresa believed that if you took care of your small responsibilities, life would reward you with bigger responsibilities. She was a doer. Her mantra was: If something needs washing, wash it. If something needs fixing, fix it. If a letter needs writing, write it. She was on top of everything. If something needed to get done immediately, she just did it.

Find Joy

It wasn't just discipline, but the joy of discipline that was striking about Mother Teresa. She found tremendous joy in her daily work. She was filled with vitality deeply rooted in her inner happiness. Even at 6a.m. she was smiling, rejuvenating those around her. She relished the challenges of running a global organization.

How did Mother Teresa stay motivated? Was she just naturally iron-willed, indefatigable, immune to temptation? Didn't she have down days where the mountain just seemed too high to climb, the burdens too heavy to shoulder? Where did she find the strength to smile at each person she met, and how did she radiate an aura of contentment while driving a sense of urgency? Of course, Mother Teresa was as human as the rest of us. So why was she filled with this constant vitality and inner happiness?

RUMA'S STORY: As a nineteen-year-old, I saw Mother Teresa as superhuman. I asked her how she did it. Patient as always, she told me about the relationship of discipline and joy. Something about the concept of finding happiness in discipline was foreign to me. But Mother Teresa used the joy of discipline to turn necessary tasks into motivating moments of pleasure, and to refill her seemingly endless reserves of energy and happiness.

Practice

The joy of discipline starts with understanding that discipline is a practice. Like any practice, to be effective it must be repeated. It develops character, skills, and endurance. But repetition can lead to boredom, and little by little practice becomes monotony. It is at this point that willpower can fade, and boredom becomes the first excuse to get off track.

The joy of discipline counters this inevitable erosion of focus by reminding us to take pleasure and quiet pride in trying, in the simple act of engaging in the practice each day. Mother Teresa believed God wants us to try, whether or not we succeed. So we must find the joy in everything we do, in the very fact of trying, without judging by the final result.

RUMA'S STORY: I have committed to running. I love what it does for my body, my mind, and my spirit. Of course, no matter how I plan my days, at some point I will have a conflict between my planned run and an emergency at work, a friend in need, lethargy, or a myriad of other excuses that my mind devises. It is so easy to rationalize skipping the run. I don't have enough time to do my whole route today, so why not wait until I can do it right?

By applying Mother Teresa's joy of discipline, I get a different answer: Just run today, even a little, and be happy with myself for keeping the discipline. The purpose of the discipline for me is to prepare for a half marathon, and faithfulness to the discipline gives me the joy of knowing I am still preparing, still trying. Next time it is time to run, I remember the joy I get from the effort, the joy of discipline, and I can't wait to head out the door and experience it again. I take pleasure in my work, knowing its value.

Mother Teresa shows us that in addition to the joy of discipline, we can use the discipline of joy to generate energy in ourselves and those around us. The discipline of joy is the regular practice of enjoying what we love, with those we love. Its simplest form is a smile. This one simple act is infectious, generating joy for everyone involved. Mother Teresa, in her letter to me as a child, reminded me to smile at the old man. For her, a smile was an act of love.

Many leaders think there is no practical place for joy in business, that it may even be counterproductive. We may hesitate to look for joy in our work because we fear being seen as weak, idle, or lacking in commitment. Often we act serious and even grim to make sure everyone knows we take our responsibilities seriously. We play the role of the serious ant, grimly preparing to survive the coming winter, while failing to notice that our energy is waning and our followers are going through the motions. But, as Mother Teresa knew and practiced, it is joy, not only willpower or commitment, that keeps us going and moves others to go with us. To find joy consistently is itself a practice, the discipline of joy.

A former colleague of Ruma's, a serial entrepreneur in the hypercompetitive software industry, said that if you aren't having fun, you aren't taking the job seriously enough. His point was that success is a marathon, and to run a marathon, one needs fuel. Joy is the fuel that keeps us running through the pain of effort and the loneliness of doubt. And while joy can't be forced, it can be encouraged through practice. By taking time every day to laugh with colleagues, relax with friends, and open ourselves to beauty, we practice the discipline of joy.

LOU'S STORY: In the companies I run, I often create a "Quote Book" in which I write down the accidentally funny things that people say at work. Over time people really get into the fun of the Quote Book. They actually start to compete to make it into the book. This simple device helps people make sure we don't always take ourselves too seriously and brings laughter and joy into the organization.

Mother Teresa knew that joy is the foundation for success, and that as such it cannot be left to chance. We are at our best when practicing both the joy of discipline and the discipline of joy, accepting the happiness that comes from consistently trying even when it is hard, and finding the fuel of happiness that we all need to do great things together.

THE TERESA PRINCIPLES

Discover the Joy of Discipline
- If it can be done now, do it now
- Practice discipline
- Take your work seriously, never yourself
- Seek joy in all you do

CHAPTER SIX

Communicate in a Language People Understand

Do ordinary things with extraordinary love.

MOTHER TERESA

The first person to bring Mother Teresa and her work to the broader attention of the Western world was British journalist Malcolm Muggeridge. In 1970 he filmed an inspiring documentary for the BBC called *Something Beautiful for God,* which was aired by most European and American TV stations. He went on to write a book about Mother Teresa. The public's response to Muggeridge's documentary and book was immediate and widespread.

Many other people, then and since, have worked tirelessly to help the poor. What was so unusually compelling about Mother Teresa's story? One thing was the way she herself told it. Mother Teresa was able to persuade most people to see things her way. Her ability to converse with anyone from politicians, dignitaries, journalists, and world leaders to the poorest beggars in the street was one of her great secrets of success.

Mother Teresa did not know many languages, but when it came to communicating, she was an expert. If there were such a thing as a universal language, it would be what Mother Teresa spoke. The purity and simplicity with which she communicated transcended language barriers. She spoke with her voice, her eyes, her ears, and her heart. Her most eloquent way of communicating was through her smile. "Peace begins with a smile," she often said. She could also touch you deeply with her words, no matter how simple they were or how short the time.

Connection

Mother Teresa always had time for people—all people. If you took the time to come and visit her in Calcutta, she took the time to greet you. A little sign by the main door of the motherhouse said, "Visiting Hours (for Mother) 8a.m. to 12 Noon, 3p.m. to 6p.m. No Visitors on Thursday." But if you knocked at the door outside of visiting hours, a sister would greet you warmly, and if Mother Teresa was available, she would come and say hello. She would ask about you. She would sit with you, envelop your hands in hers, look deeply into your eyes, let you get lost in dialogue, and listen. She would provide you with insight, usually what you needed to hear in that moment. She would tell you about the work of the missions and encourage you to visit them and volunteer. She would make you feel important for those few minutes. And you would remember that moment forever.

RUMA'S STORY: People came from practically every country on the planet to see Mother Teresa, and she connected to each and every person, despite language barriers. I remember one day, after Mass, seeing a group of Japanese businessmen waiting quietly for her. They seemed very powerful and stoic. They didn't have an interpreter, and they didn't speak English. The moment Mother entered, I watched their expressions elevate, and they began to bow repeatedly. Mother Teresa stood graciously and smiled. I walked by a few moments later, and I saw everyone smiling and laughing. There was meaningful communication with no words. It was simple, it was short, and it was transformative.

Understanding Your Audience

Mother Teresa faced daunting communication challenges. She knew that the Missionaries of Charity, like any organization, is only as strong as the information and inspiration flowing through its communication channels. But how could she communicate everything from grand vision to small operational details across the barriers of distance, language, background, differing agendas, illness, and pain? Her approach was simple and powerful: communicate in a language people understand.

How did she know how to speak to different people at different times in different ways? How did she always make people feel she understood them and "spoke" their language?

Part of the answer was her authenticity. Her love for humankind was embedded in everything she said. Her hearers felt the authenticity of her dialogue. She also had empathy and compassion.

Many people approach communication as a matter of consistency, clarity, and presentation style. They have a message to convey, and they feel the only way to make sure it is received is to carefully craft the words, then repeatedly present them in a consistent style. The unspoken assumption is that the speaker is too important to adapt to the audience, much less listen to it.

Mother Teresa took the opposite approach. To her, communication was often more about listening and observing than about speaking. By first listening with kind attention and a genuine desire to understand, instead of an urgent need to push her message, she could learn her listeners' true language from words, tone of voice, gestures, breathing, cadence, body language, and eye contact. She used this information to adapt her language, naturally but intentionally, to that of other people, while paying close attention to their responses. Did they understand what she was really saying? Were they open to her words and intentions? Did she need to stop and listen some more?

Through focused attention, active listening, and adaptation, Mother Teresa consistently spoke in a language that her listeners understood, even if they did not share many common words or came from very different backgrounds. By understanding her audience, she could speak to them in a manner that resonated with them. Her words always came from the heart but were specific to the person in front of her. Regardless of the content of the message, and of her considerable authority, she communicated as one human to another. She trusted her instincts and skills, the power of her vision, and the good intentions of the other party, rather than relying on rehearsed phrases and standardized presentation.

It takes courage to communicate in the language of others. Formal training in various communication styles, including observation and practice, can help. But the key to effective communication is recognizing the uniqueness of each individual, then having the courage and the skill to adapt your language to that person's needs.

It is not a matter of becoming, or masquerading as, someone you are not, but of being who you truly are in a way the other person can understand. This demands cultivating an authentic, personal voice but contextualizing your message with your audience in mind at all times. It requires empathy, and empathy necessitates awareness of and sensitivity to your audience's feelings and personality. Within that understanding, find your own voice.

It can be hard to see how to apply Mother Teresa's communication principle in business. How does it work when making a sales or fund-raising pitch to a group of strangers? Talking to analysts, investors, or the public about a bad quarter? Terminating an employee? Communicating in writing?

Each of these situations poses a different communication challenge. Some seem to call for a careful choice of "safe" words to avoid possible misunderstanding or claims of harm. In others, it would be easier to deliver a quick, one-sided message and move on. Even in these challenging cases, however, the principle can be applied.

First, stop. Remind yourself that your message is not worth anything unless it is understood. If you have not met the other person, use your imagination. For practical inspiration, read Warren Buffett's annual letter to shareholders of Berkshire Hathaway—a formal, written document for a mass audience that somehow manages to speak plainly and directly to each person who reads it.

Second, remind yourself of the vision. The dream contains something universal to both parties, or you wouldn't be communicating. You have common ground, even if the conversation is one-way.

Third, pay attention to your surroundings and feelings. If you aren't speaking in a language that fits the situation and expresses your intentions, you probably aren't speaking in your listener's language either.

Last, reflect on your intentions. Kind intentions, even in tough situations, increase the chances of trust. And if you are not trusted, you will rarely be understood.

It can get incredibly frustrating when you communicate with someone who speaks a different language or whose message you don't understand. To avoid this, you need to know your listeners and analyze how you interact with them, be they employees, customers, vendors, or regulators. Be aware of how you communicate. Listen carefully to your audience and align your communication style with theirs. Keep to your message, but be ready to alter the way you connect. Your goal is successfully communicating your message, not communicating it in a particular way.

If a leader has the courage and skill to communicate in a language people understand, the echoes of that communication will reverberate as clarity, collaboration, and confidence throughout the organization.

RUMA'S STORY: While I was traveling in India a few years ago, I found myself seduced by the lure of buying a silk rug. I had done some research and knew exactly what style of carpet I wanted. I was very excited by the thought of my purchase! I went to a local rug merchant and tried to explain to the salesperson what, specifically, I wanted. Unfortunately, he spoke little English and I spoke little Hindi. Given that I was the customer, I decided English was going to be our language of communication. As I tried to explain myself, the salesperson's face was blank. I assumed he wasn't listening to me, so I proceeded to raise my voice louder and louder, to no avail. This strategy obviously failed because he didn't understand English, and it left both of us extremely frustrated. What I should have done was communicate in a language he did understand. I should have brought pictures, drawn the design, showed him colors, gestured to carpets I liked in the store, with a calm and friendly demeanor. Instead, I created an uncomfortable scene that didn't accomplish my mission of buying a carpet. I returned the next day with my new approach and walked out with a carpet I enjoy to this day. This type of frustration is not uncommon when we try to communicate with someone who doesn't understand us.

Communication Styles

We all have our own styles of communicating. How do your employees react to your style? Do they deliver on the tasks you have assigned? What about your parents, spouse, or siblings? Do you communicate in a different way with family than with colleagues or customers? Has more than one person told you that you are too aggressive, not clear enough, too soft-spoken, or sometimes confusing? This kind of feedback is a gift, so use it. If you have ever been frustrated trying to communicate something when the other person "just didn't get it," then try changing your style of communication.

A good business professional adjusts to other people's styles. Good politicians are masters of this. Determining where you need to adapt requires observing other people's styles. Are they low-context, requiring details and step-by-step instructions? Perhaps they are visual, requiring charts or other visual aids to understand. Do they deliver more successfully when they are armed with examples, or do they like to work their own way based on knowing the end goal? Figuring these things out isn't easy, and the answers aren't always obvious. People won't tell you their style, and they don't always give and receive information in the same way. You have to learn by having empathy for your audience, keenly observing the hints (often body language) that they give you about their style, reflecting on what was successful, and truly wanting to communicate your message.

RUMA'S STORY: As co-CEO and president of a consumer products company, I knew proper communication of our core message was a key driver of the success of our brand. As we began to scale our business, we decided to align our brand with a celebrity who espoused similar values. In pursuit of that goal, I found myself pitching to an artist's team for both an endorsement and an investment from the artist's investment fund. These are two very different goals, so I found myself in a meeting with three people with different objectives. The artist's manager was looking to get as much money as possible for an endorsement; the head of the artist's investment fund and his chief operating officer were looking to see a scalable business with potential for a successful exit and return.

The challenge of delivering a message to a group with different objectives is tailoring it to each person's needs. As I prepared for the meeting, I thought through the general attributes of people in those positions, what would be important to them, and how they would like to receive information. Then, during the formal introductions, I observed and listened carefully for insights into their personalities and styles. I knew I had to highlight the benefits to each of them to successfully raise money from one side and get an endorsement from the other. As I addressed each person, I switched the way I conveyed my message.

The artist's manager was focused on maintaining the right image based on the artist's core values. She shared many stories and made comments about the artist's foundation. When addressing her, I highlighted our brand values and demonstrated how our philosophies were aligned with those of the foundation. I gave examples of how we could collaborate and develop joint campaigns that focused on the foundation's work. One example involved developing a product specifically for a cause important to the artist and donating a percentage of revenue to her foundation. My key message was, "We care about what you care about."

The investment folks, however, were more interested in the return on investment. Their questions were all data-driven. They were interested in the details. They wanted to know how much things cost, how things got financed, and how all this affected cash flow and the bottom line. I only had one hour, and I knew I would lose the interest of the manager if I focused solely on in-depth financials, which did not directly affect her. I made sure to clearly answer the questions within a framework based on data, and I offered the fund representatives more time to discuss the details after the meeting. By taking this approach, I addressed their questions but did not lose the manager's interest.

Each of these people needed to receive and relate to the presentation in a language he or she understood. The key was presenting the information within a framework of how each person liked to receive information. The artist's manager spoke to me with stories, emotions, and examples; the investment people spoke to me with data, facts, and comparables. I communicated the same brand message tailored to each of them in the manner they understood—stories and examples, data and comparables. In the end, all sides felt heard, and the meeting was very productive.

LOU'S STORY: As the CEO of a rapidly growing software company, I needed everyone in the organization to understand how it made money and how each of them individually contributed to it. To accomplish this, we had to talk to over five hundred people, with all kinds of backgrounds, in the languages they understood. While the financial people understood the numbers and how we made money, generally the engineers did not. We had to lay a foundation for the necessary learning. At a series of employee meetings, we discussed the numbers: how they came to be and what each one meant. By the end of our program, the engineers were often asking tougher questions about the numbers than the directors were.

Mother Teresa probably didn't analyze her communication style. She did not have a speechwriter, a media consultant, or a coach. She listened actively because she had empathy for people and wanted to understand their needs. Whether she was serving the poor directly, speaking to a politician, or raising money from a CEO, she always left her imprint by communicating in a language that the other person understood.

THE TERESA PRINCIPLES

Communication in a Language People Understand
- Be authentic
- Know your audience
- Listen and show empathy
- Adjust your communication style to the other person

CHAPTER SEVEN

Pay Attention to the Janitor

*Be generous and understanding.
Let no one come to you without feeling
better and happier when they leave.
Be the living expression of God's kindness:
with kindness on your face, kindness in
your eyes, kindness in your smile,
kindness in your warm greeting.*

MOTHER TERESA

Journalisth Dan Wooding once wrote, "The other day, a friend asked me which of the thousands of interviews I have done over the years had impacted me the most. That was an easy one to answer. It was with Mother Teresa of Calcutta, the 'Saint of the Gutters.'"[12] Countless other journalists have made similar statements.

One reason Mother Teresa touched people so deeply was that she made them feel heard and valued. She understood that at the most basic level, we all want to feel valued in what we do, whether by our families, our friends, or our colleagues.

As mentioned earlier, Mother Teresa opened many homes for the dying, the desolate, and the destitute. She believed that everyone should feel valued enough to pass away in peace, surrounded by warmth and love. As she put it, "My years of dedication and service to the poor have helped me to understand that it is precisely they who really understand human dignity. Their main problem is not their lack of money but the fact that their right to be treated humanely and lovingly is not recognized."[13]

Mother Teresa also knew that valuing people could change their lives. Mrs. Ann Blaikie, cochair of the International Association of Mother Teresa's Co-Workers, told this story:

One day as we were walking with Mother Teresa along the streets of Calcutta, a young man dashed up to us and knelt down to kiss Mother Teresa's feet. He told her that he was going to be married in a few hours. Mother Teresa explained to me that, a few months before, the young man had been brought, dying from hunger and tuberculosis, to the home for the dying. At the house he had been cared for and had learned a modest occupation, that of shining shoes. It had been enough to enable him to start a new life.[14]

Never Forget the People Who Helped You on Your Life Journey

Life is a journey filled with stories—some happy, some sad, and many in between. Throughout this journey we meet people who influence and help us in multiple ways. Some remain friends, others come in and out of our lives, and many go away. It is important to be grateful and remember those who have touched our lives along the way. They were gifts given to us. Think about who these people have been in your life and give a moment of thanks.

In 1979 Mother Teresa received the Nobel Peace Prize. She chose to bring with her to Stockholm the first two sisters who had had the courage to leave the Sisters of Loreto with her to start a new life. That sense of appreciation and gratitude was apparent in her every word, task, and thought.

Pay Attention!

How do you make people feel valued? Pay attention to them! Acknowledge who they are. Ask them questions. Know their names. If you are a leader in your organization, take the time to remember the names of all the people you meet. Acknowledge them, or you may never learn what they have to offer. If you judge people by title or reputation, without trying to get to know them, then you'll never know what they have to offer, and you could miss out on a valuable opportunity.

RUMA'S STORY: The first time I met Mother Teresa, she lovingly enveloped my hands in hers and made me feel like I was the most important person for her at that moment. She felt so powerful, and yet so tender. That first moment remains vivid in my mind.

Mother Teresa seemed to hear hearts and see into souls. She created a safe environment that fostered intense dialogue and soul searching with no fear of judgment. Her sincerity made everyone feel valued, and her warmth and love carried those who met her into another state of mind. I had the immense, humbling privilege of seeing this magical transformation over and over again. Her magic was human and contagious, and her language was universal love. She treated everyone with the same respect—a child in the slums, an AIDS patient in New York, or a corporate executive. She believed we all have the ability to connect to others in the purest way. That simple human magic was her spiritual bedrock, the foundation of her vision and her organization.

Mother Teresa always greeted people the same way. As you interact with the people in your company, do you engage with them all in the same way? Or do you talk one way with the janitor and a completely different way with your senior executives? You already know the answers. If you really are not sure, think about what others would say if they saw you engaging with different people in your organization. Could they tell the difference?

Mother Teresa led the way with her behavior, and the sisters tried to emulate her. Mother Teresa was the change she wanted to be in her organization. It started with her and became inherent in the way everyone in the Missionaries of Charity treated people. You can have the same effect in your organization with your behavior.

LOU'S STORY: One lesson I learned from my dad is to give everyone in your organization the same respect. My dad believed that the people in the mail room know their role in the company better than anyone else and thus are in the best position to know how to improve it. My dad taught me to listen to them as I would to a senior executive, as both have value as people and value to add to the organization. This lesson opened me up to be receptive to ideas from all parts of the organization. I try to apply it wherever I work.

While I was a vice president at an investment banking firm, I got into the elevator one day, and the CEO got in as well. This man was a legend on Wall Street. He turned to me, introduced himself, and asked my name and what I did at the firm. I stammered some response and was grateful when the elevator door opened and he got out, saying it was good to meet me. I learned from that moment that if the CEO cares enough about each person to ask who he is and what he does, then as a manager I had better care too. I had better care in the same way, and I had better ask and listen to those I work with, whether they are in the elevator, on the shop floor, or in the executive suite. This interaction has made me more conscious to this day about others in the organization and the contribution they each make.

Valuing your stakeholders is rewarded by loyalty, productivity, efficiency, low turnover, trust, community and investor support, and increased sales. Having a workforce of people who care about each other will translate into a great work environment and superior customer service. These in turn will lead to financial success and move you toward realizing your vision.

Mother Teresa understood this. Her kindness ranged far and wide, and years after her death, her impact continues through those she touched. She always paid attention to the janitor.

THE TERESA PRINCIPLES

Pay Attention to the Janitor
- Treat each person with respect
- Each of us wants to feel valued
- The title never matters, the person always does

CHAPTER EIGHT

Use the Power of Silence

*Love should be in season all year long
and within the reach of everyone.
Everyone can harvest love without limit.
Everyone can obtain this love through
meditation, a spirit of prayer and sacrifice,
through an intense inner life.*

MOTHER TERESA

RUMA'S STORY: The chapel on the second floor of the motherhouse was where I learned the power of silence. Every day, after Mass at 6a.m., all the sisters would gather and welcome volunteers and visitors from around the world. On any given day, there could have been people from thirty different countries, sitting quietly and praying together. There were no pews, no gold-encrusted altar, no artwork. One cross hung above the altar, and two simple candles burned on each side. If you didn't know where Mother was sitting, you wouldn't know that she was there. She would be very focused on her prayers.

For me, the act of quieting my mind was powerful. It brought me serenity and clarity of thought and purpose. It allowed me the time to be thankful and to think. This did not happen immediately, however. The windows of the chapel always remained open, letting in the cacophony of a typical Calcutta morning. As a newcomer, I found this fully tested my ability to concentrate. My mind would go straight to the distraction. If it wasn't the ambient noise, I was convinced that it was someone's cough, or the temperature, that was at fault for my mind's inability to focus. I'd watch Mother and the other sisters and see that nothing caused them to stir. When I asked Mother how she did it, she told me that she focused on God and that whenever my mind got distracted, I needed to bring it back to God. I understood what Mother was saying, and with time, I learned to discipline my mind to block the noise and focus my thoughts in the moment.

I continue to practice this kind of meditation to this day. It gives me the strength to recognize that many of the answers I need lie within me, if I take the time to listen to myself. It also gives me a sense of daily rejuvenation. I live in New York City, and I barely sleep. My early mornings are now the time I give to myself to just "be." What a turnaround! Mornings have transformed from a time of stress, when I am overwhelmed by the perceived daunting requirements of the day, to a time to be grateful for my life and the beauty around me. Meditation calms me, and that helps me understand what is truly important to accomplish that day. Practicing it daily keeps my spirit strong.

Prayer or quiet time was very, very important for Mother Teresa and her order. She saw Mass and prayer as times to be introspective, to reflect, to listen to oneself, and to listen to God. They were periods of renewal that helped her continue to show the love she had for, and the joy she felt in, her fellow human beings. In her words, "The more we are able to store up in our hearts through silent prayer, the more we will be able to give out in our work. We need silence in order to be able to touch people. The essential thing is not what we say but what God says to us and through us. All our words will be useless if they don't come from inside."[15]

Based on her experience communing with God, Mother Teresa wrote extensively on the importance of silence:

In silence we will find new energy and true unity. Silence gives us a new outlook on everything. The essential thing is not what we say but what God says to us and through us. In that silence, He will listen to us; there He will speak to our soul, and there we will hear His voice. Listen in silence because if your heart is full of other things you cannot hear the voice of God.... We cannot find God in noise or agitation. In nature we find silence—the trees, flowers, and grass grow in silence. The stars, the moon, and the sun move in silence. Silence of the heart is necessary so you can hear God everywhere—in the closing of a door, in the person who needs you, in the birds that sing, in the flowers, in the animals.... In silence He listens to us; in silence He speaks to our souls. In silence we are granted the privilege of listening to His voice.... To make possible true inner silence, practice: Silence of the eyes.... Silence of the ears.... Silence of the tongue.... Silence of the mind.... Silence of the heart.[16]

For a leader, applying the power of silence means clearing your mind and listening to your inner voice. Silence of the mind—stopping your mind—is critical. At times more difficult decisions will be coming at you than you think you can handle. Some people call this condition "information overload." Making decisions is a daily component of leadership, so you need a way to make them. Silencing your mind relieves you of mental clutter and gives you the clarity to hear your inner voice's answer.

To silence your mind, begin by eliminating all external distractions. If you are in your office, close the door and turn off all devices that could be distracting, such as your cell phone. All your messages will be there when you are done, and the voicemail service will answer your calls. If you have an assistant, tell him or her that you do not want to be disturbed unless it is a matter of life or death. It rarely is. If you are so important that you can't take even ten minutes for this process, you have other issues to address.

Once you have established a quiet environment, let all your questions wash over you. Take a backseat and give your thoughts a few minutes to fight amongst themselves for your mind's attention. One issue will likely "yell" louder than the rest. This is the first one to put your mind to solving. Think the issue through until you make a decision on it. Repeat this process one issue at a time until there are no decisions left to be made.

If you find yourself letting all the issues fight for your attention again, then stop yourself, go back to the beginning of the process, and start again. Over time this process will become second nature, and you will be able to reach a silence of the mind quickly and easily. Don't be surprised or concerned if at times you revert to your old behaviors and begin to feel completely overwhelmed again. Stop. Then actively start the process again.

LOU'S STORY: When I had just become the CEO of a software company, a senior executive of our largest single customer, a multibillion-dollar global company, told me it was terminating our agreement because our company was in breach of it. This termination would have devastated our company.

Late that night I was finally able to get to a place of no distraction. I then worked to silence my mind, acknowledging each extraneous issue that came to me and then letting go of it for the time being. Because I had so many issues fighting for my attention, this process took a long time. I thought about how losing this relationship would mean having to eliminate a large number of jobs, regardless of the performance of the people in them; I thought of how our investors would feel about the value of the company being severely reduced; I thought of how it would impact my future. Ultimately, however, I was able to quiet my mind.

I was then free to focus on the issue itself. I did this by figuratively holding it in my hands and turning it many different ways, looking at it as I did so. This process enabled me to see it from new perspectives. Over time, I began to see a potential strategy to attempt to get this relationship back on a strong foundation. After returning to the office, I laid out the strategy, and we began to implement it aggressively. Through the combined efforts of a great team of people, we ultimately were able to resolve the issue and continue this business relationship. Had I not been able to silence my mind and get enough space to thoughtfully address this issue, our company and the people in it would have suffered.

If you take time to silence your mind regularly, your mind will find the answers you need for every aspect of your life.

THE TERESA PRINCIPLES

Use the Power of Silence
- Silence is about stopping
- Stop your talking—listen
- Stop your mind—be thoughtful
- Silence your heart—love

CONCLUSION

You Don't Have to Be a Saint

You don't have to be a saint to benefit from Mother Teresa's leadership principles. They can and should be used by anyone seeking to build a great organization. They can be applied every day to improve how your organization works. The balanced application of a simple, clear vision, practical trade-offs, patience, inquiry, joyful discipline, true communication, equal regard, and silent reflection provides a practical framework that leaders can choose now, with immediate results. These principles will improve performance at all levels of your organization and in all phases of your business or your life. They will work for you whether you are the president of a great nation, the CEO of a multinational corporation, the executive director of a nonprofit or an NGO, the manager of a branch office, or a parent, teacher, or volunteer. Our inspiration is the hope that Mother Teresa's leadership principles may touch your life in some way, great or small. If they do, you have our thanks, and this book has accomplished its purpose.

RUMA'S STORY: During my time as a volunteer with the Missionaries of Charity, my focus was on the here and now. There was work to be done, every day. And I had my own issues to struggle through. If you had asked me then what I was learning about business, I would not have known what you were talking about.

Nearly twenty years later, I realize that I was in the presence not only of spiritual greatness, but also of executive excellence. My business education and entrepreneurial experience have hammered home one truth over and over: creating a great enterprise, especially at scale, is incredibly difficult, and never happens by chance. Creating the Missionaries of Charity—founding it, nurturing it, and growing it to a global organization with millions of workers, tens of millions of clients, and billions of dollars of capital—ranks among the great business accomplishments in human history. The organization's survival is testimony to Mother Teresa's vision and tenacity. Its continued vibrant growth after her death speaks to an even greater accomplishment and tells us that there was more at work than one considerable personality.

As I have worked to create my own businesses, and to help others with theirs, I have found myself intuitively returning to my time with the Missionaries of Charity and asking, How? How did she do it? What principles did she apply to create an organization that bore the stamp of her personality, but transcended her individuality?

Finally, after fifteen years of immersion in the business world, the light switched on for me. In a single conversation, when asked what Mother Teresa's management secrets were, I found myself describing the concepts that are embodied in this book:

PRINCIPLE 1: Dream it simple, say it strong—
Create a vision that is simple. Say it
strongly with words and actions at every
possible moment.

PRINCIPLE 2: To get to the angels, deal with
 the devil—
Develop a framework to make decisions
on ethical issues.

PRINCIPLE 3: Wait! Then pick your moment—
Before beginning, be prepared emotionally,
financially, and operationally.

PRINCIPLE 4: Embrace the power of doubt—
Relentlessly question your business.

PRINCIPLE 5: Discover the joy of discipline—
Discipline can bring you joy.

PRINCIPLE 6: Communicate in a language people
understand.

PRINCIPLE 7: Pay attention to the janitor—
Everyone has value.

PRINCIPLE 8: Use the power of silence—

Calm your mind and listen.

Mother Teresa did the seemingly impossible by consistently applying a set of timeless management principles to the problem of serving the poorest of the poor. She did so in a thoughtful and balanced way, never letting the principles become dogma, and never letting one principle dominate the others. As I reflected further, it became clear to me that these principles not only made sense decades ago when she founded the Missionaries of Charity, but are even more applicable in today's highly interconnected world of business. And as part of my calling, I was compelled to write this book.

Last year was my time to act. This book is a result of that action—nearly twenty years after my experience. It took Mother Teresa nearly twenty years to start the Missionaries of Charity.

When is your time? Has it come? What are you the Mother Teresa of?

Start today by picking one principle that resonates with you. Implement it and begin to change how you lead your life or your organization. It will make a difference.

Then take the next principle that you are drawn to, much as Mother Teresa was drawn to serving the poorest of the poor. Implement that principle.

Simply continue at the pace at which you are comfortable, but never get too comfortable in just one place. Leadership is never about complacency.

Within one month of taking action, you will be achieving results that you have never thought possible. You will notice the difference.

Like Mother Teresa, you have been called to action. Act.

***

We would love to hear your stories about how you have used Mother Teresa's principles to change the leadership of your organization or your own life. Please send your stories to MyChanges@mtleadership.com , where we will share them with others so that they may learn from your leadership as well. Thank you.

At the moment of death we will not be judged according to the number of good deeds we have done or by the diplomas we have received in our lifetime. We will be judged according to the love we have put into our work.
MOTHER TERESA

The Missionaries of Charity Today

Mother Teresa left this earth in 1997. She appointed Sister Mary Nirmala Joshi to succeed her in leading the Missionaries of Charity into the next century. In 2009, Sister Nirmala was succeeded by Sister Mary Prema. Since Mother Teresa's death, the Missionaries of Charity have added 163 houses in eleven countries on five continents, totaling 757 centers in 134 countries so far.

RUMA'S STORY: The sisters continue to be guided by the principles lived by their founder. I recently went back to Calcutta to see how things operated without her presence, and I found her spirit and legacy living on through the next generation of sisters. I observed through dialogue that their decision-making process was founded on the question, "What would Mother do?"

I had the pleasure of interacting with volunteers after Mass one December morning, and it brought me back to my 1992 experience. I heard multiple languages around me. There must have been over fifty people from at least twenty-five different countries. I met with a mother and daughter from Rochester, New York, a brother and sister from Barcelona, two best friends from France, and others from all age groups and walks of life. The two sisters in charge of the volunteers were Korean and Spanish, and the management process was exactly as it had been before: organized, thoughtful, and inspiring.

The day I visited was the last day for one of the volunteers, a girl of no more than twenty-four. She came to the front of the room while everyone else sang, "Thank you, thank you, thank you..." It was heartfelt and warm and reminded me of the importance of acknowledging people and being grateful.

If you would like to volunteer and experience the terrific work of the Sisters of Charity in Calcutta, you can start at 3p.m. on any Monday, Wednesday, or Friday. Just go to an orientation at the Shisu Bhavan orphanage, down the street from the motherhouse at 54A A.J.C. Bose Road, across from the big red tax building. They welcome all volunteers, for as long or as short a time as you'd like. For more information, you can visit the official website at http://www.moth erteresacenter.org.

Like any nonprofit organization, the Missionaries of Charity are able to do their work because of generous donations from individuals like you and me. If you would like to support the legacy of Mother Teresa, please take the time to find a center near you and give!

Notes

[1] Mother Teresa Center's official website: http://www.motherteresa.org/. The Missionaries of Charity does not disclose either the sources of its funds or details of how they are spent. The organization falls under a special provision of Indian law. Consequently, the amount of capital raised is an estimate.

[2] http://en.wikipedia.org/wiki/Missionaries_of_Charity.

[3] http://en.wikipedia.org/wiki/Mother_Teresa.

[4] Mother Teresa Center's official website: http://www.motherteresa.org/ .

[5] Christopher Hitchens, *The Missionary Position: Mother Teresa in Theory and Practice* (London: Verso, 1995).

[6] Ibid.

[7] *Stern,* September 10, 1998.

[8] http://www.texnews.com/1998/religion/morph0117.html , January 17, 1998.

[9] José Luis González-Balado, comp., *Mother Teresa: In My Own Words* (New York: Gramercy Books, 1996).

[10] Brian Kolodiejchuk, M.C., ed., *Mother Teresa: Come Be My Light—The Private Writings of the "Saint of Calcutta"* (New York: Doubleday, 2007).

[11] Ambrose Redmoon, "No Peaceful Warriors!" *Gnosis: A Journal of the Western Inner Traditions* 21 (Fall 1991).

[12] http://www.assistnews.net/Stories/2010/s100 70019.htm.

[13] José Luis González-Balado, *Stories of Mother Teresa: Her Smile and Her Words* (Liguori Publications, 1983).

[14] Ibid.

[15] Ibid.

[16] Mother Teresa, *In the Heart of the World,* ed. Becky Benenate (Novato, Calif.: New World Library), quoted at http://www.newworldlibrary .com/ArticleDetails/tabid/230/ArticleID/168/D efault.aspx.

Acknowledgments

RUMA: I have so much to be thankful for. Completing this book over these last two years has been an incredible experience for me.

I wrote this book because my journey is like every woman's—I am a seeker, a woman in transition, trying to find my own path to improving the world. The time I spent with Mother Teresa changed my life forever. I wanted to share that, hoping my journey might offer inspiration for others.

Writing a book was much harder than I could ever have imagined! I am thankful to the entire team at Berrett-Koehler, especially Steve Piersanti and Jeevan Sivasubramaniam, for their enthusiasm about our project and constant support. Thank you also to Lynn Golbetz for her excellent copy editing.

I have been blessed with great friends, who have doubled as editors and given me emotional support throughout this process. I am very grateful to all of you and apologize if I have left your names out.

I'd like to thank Lou, my mentor, my friend, and my coauthor, who has been an anchor in my life since he entered my world. I'd also like to thank Julie Lazarus for being the catalyst that began this incredible journey; Katie Gilligan for generously holding my hand and guiding me through the publishing world; Jeff Wald for encouraging me to go for it; Philip Kiracofe for your helpful introductions and constant support; Chris Beall, Rebecca Eaton, and

Linda Gottlieb for your tremendous editorial help; Monica Mehta for giving me the biweekly encouragement to stick with this; Brian Subirana for your intellectual support; Phyllis Wender for your sage advice; and Leonie Maruani, Jacqui Holmes, Vanu Bose, Tanya Kostic, Anjula Acharia Bath, Ian Warburg, Imran Sayeed, Deirdre Evans, Sanjoy Chatterjee, Doug Chertok, Scott Morris, Tracey Matchett, Ajay Desai, Neil Patel, Vernand Morency, Laurie Meadoff, Arun Singh, and Stephane Bibeau for being encouraging friends through different stages of the process. Special thanks to Krishna Sondhi and Ian Mayo-Smith for your love and guidance and encouragement to write this book, Akshay Mansukhani for always being the supportive little brother, Jean Zimmerman for inviting me into your life and being an inspirational role model, Rana Lahiry for your friendship and stepping in as a father figure when I lost mine, and Aasif Mandvi for making me a better person and helping me find my voice.

The foundation of who I am is the spiritual strength I have gained from my mother. Were it not for her value system and belief in me, I would never have gained a perspective that would lead me down this path. I am thankful every day for her presence in my life. Dad, if I had one more day with you, I would thank you and let you know how proud I am of you. Your spirit lives within me every day. Finally, Simon, you are too young today to recognize the tremendous joy you bring into my life, but I hope when you are older, you know how much happiness a simple smile or phone call from you brings me.

LOU: I am thankful to have been a part of creating this book, and that is due to Ruma. My role in all of this has been a simple one: help give voice to the story of two remarkable women—Mother Teresa, an iconic global leader whose timeless principles we can all learn from and put to use in our lives and in running our companies, and Ruma Bose, also a remarkable woman making her own indelible mark on those people and organizations she touches, wherever in the world they may be.

Inevitably people are forgotten when individuals are acknowledged in the creation of a book. It is truly an amazing, collaborative endeavor and a lot more work than I could ever have imagined. I would like to thank the great team we were fortunate to work with at Berrett-Koehler, from Steve Piersanti to Jeevan Sivasubramaniam, as well as the entire marketing, sales, and production team at BK, including Lynn Golbetz. I am also eternally thankful to the many friends who helped, encouraged, and inquired throughout the process. Any errors or omissions are solely Ruma's and mine.

On the personal side, I would like to thank my sons, Tyler and Dylan, for the lessons they teach me every day that make me a better person; Lori, their mother, for her constant love of the boys; my sisters, Barbara and Nancy, whose unquestioned support means more than I can ever say; my dad and Rusty, whose commitment to each other was unswerving; and my mom, whose spirit remains with me. Finally, I would like to give special thanks to Christine, a truly remarkable person who enabled me to look at life in new, meaningful, and beautiful ways.

About the Authors

RUMA BOSE is a serial entrepreneur, investor, philanthropist, and author. In 1992/1993, Ruma spent time in Calcutta working with Mother Teresa and the Missionaries of Charity.

Ruma is currently president and co-CEO of Spray-ology, an innovative wellness company that sells vitamin and homeopathic oral sprays.

Previously, Ruma worked as a venture capitalist, advisor, and executive at many early-stage companies in the consumer industry. She cofounded a national floor-finishing company in the janitorial services industry. She then moved to the beauty industry, where she advised several luxury brands and was president of a leading boutique cosmetics firm in New York City."

Ruma currently serves on the boards of Secret-Builders, an online children's edutainment firm. She is also an active philanthropist, advising many non-profits and serving on the boards of SEED NY, Kopernik and her Pow-Wow Foundation.

LOUIS FAUST III is a businessman with more than thirty years of experience. He is the managing partner and founder of Edge Capital Partners, LLC, founded in 1996 to provide strategic advice to emerging growth companies.

Prior to that, Lou retired from Salomon Brothers after a ten-year career culminating in positions as a managing director and the head of global operations. He worked for Salomon Brothers in Japan from 1989 through 1994, beginning as CFO for Asia and ending as the Japan branch manager. Before going to Japan, he ran the firm's worldwide planning process and its contractual products group in New York.

Over the past thirty years, Lou has held a number of board and senior management positions. He has run three institutionally funded companies and has worked with and invested in companies in a range of industries, including consumer and industrial products, business intelligence, and software. He enjoys travel, reading, and golf, and has coauthored a golf humor book titled *Book of Mulligan: 18 Guaranteed Ways to Lower Your Golf Score Today.*

Berrett–Koehler
BK Publishers

Berrett-Koehler is an independent publisher dedicated to an ambitious mission: *Creating a World That Works for All.*

We believe that to truly create a better world, action is needed at all levels—individual, organizational, and societal. At the individual level, our publications help people align their lives with their values and with their aspirations for a better world. At the organizational level, our publications promote progressive leadership and management practices, socially responsible approaches to business, and humane and effective organizations. At the societal level, our publications advance social and economic justice, shared prosperity, sustainability, and new solutions to national and global issues.

A major theme of our publications is "Opening Up New Space." Berrett-Koehler titles challenge conventional thinking, introduce new ideas, and foster positive change. Their common quest is changing the underlying beliefs, mindsets, institutions, and structures that keep generating the same cycles of problems, no matter who our leaders are or what improvement programs we adopt.

We strive to practice what we preach—to operate our publishing company in line with the ideas in our books. At the core of our approach is stewardship, which we define as a deep sense of responsibility to administer the company for the benefit of all of our "stakeholder" groups: authors, customers, employees, investors, service providers, and the communities and environment around us.

We are grateful to the thousands of readers, authors, and other friends of the company who consider themselves to be part of the "BK Community." We hope that you, too, will join us in our mission.

A BK Business Book

This book is part of our BK Business series. BK Business titles pioneer new and progressive leadership and management practices in all types of public, private, and nonprofit organizations. They promote socially responsible approaches to business, innovative organizational change methods, and more humane and effective organizations.

Berrett–Koehler
Publishers

A community dedicated to creating
a world that works for all

Visit Our Website: www.bkconnection.com

Read book excerpts, see author videos and Internet movies, read our authors' blogs, join discussion groups, download book apps, find out about the BK Affiliate Network, browse subject-area libraries of books, get special discounts, and more!

Subscribe to Our Free E-Newsletter, the BK Communiqué

Be the first to hear about new publications, special discount offers, exclusive articles, news about bestsellers, and more! Get on the list for our free e-newsletter by going to www.bkconnection.com.

Get Quantity Discounts

Berrett-Koehler books are available at quantity discounts for orders of ten or more copies. Please call us toll-free at (800) 929-2929 or email us at bkp.orders@aidcvt.com.

Join the BK Community

BKcommunity.com is a virtual meeting place where people from around the world can engage with kindred spirits to create a world that works for all. BKcommu nity.com members may create their own profiles, blog, start and participate in forums and discussion groups, post photos and videos, answer surveys, announce and register for upcoming events, and chat with others online in real time. Please join the conversation!

108

Books For ALL Kinds of Readers

At ReadHowYouWant we understand that one size does not fit all types of readers. Our innovative, patent pending technology allows us to design new formats to make reading easier and more enjoyable for you. This helps improve your speed of reading and your comprehension. Our EasyRead printed books have been optimized to improve word recognition, ease eye tracking by adjusting word and line spacing as well as minimizing hyphenation. Our EasyRead SuperLarge editions have been developed to make reading easier and more accessible for vision-impaired readers. We offer Braille and DAISY formats of our books and all popular E-Book formats.

We are continually introducing new formats based upon research and reader preferences. Visit our web-site to see all of our formats and learn how you can Personalize our books for yourself or as gifts. Sign up to Become A RHYW Registered Reader.

www.readhowyouwant.com

Made in the USA
Middletown, DE
04 February 2015